Where Is the Congo?

by Megan Stine

illustrated by Dede Putra

Penguin Workshop

PENGUIN WORKSHOP
An Imprint of Penguin Random House LLC, New York

Visit us online at www.penguinrandomhouse.com.

Library of Congress Control Number: 2019054569

ISBN 9780593093214 (paperback)   10 9 8 7 6 5 4 3 2 1
ISBN 9780593093221 (library binding)   10 9 8 7 6 5 4 3 2 1

Contents

Where Is the Congo? 1

The Heart of Africa 7

Kingdom of Kongo 16

Stanley's Fame 27

The King Wants Cake 32

Slave Labor 44

Speaking Truth to the King 57

One Country, Many Names 68

Jungle Life 81

Saving the Congo 95

Timelines 104

Bibliography 106

Where Is the Congo?

In 1871, Henry Morton Stanley was a reporter, roaming the world and reporting back to a newspaper in the United States. Like a lot of adventurous young men, he wanted to go exploring. He also wanted to become famous. Back then, where was the best place to go to make a name for himself?

Africa!

Henry Morton Stanley

Africa was a huge continent with many different tribes and cultures. But very few

Luba people, a Bantu ethnic
group in Central Africa

Americans or Europeans had been there yet. Mistakenly, they thought it was a vast empty territory waiting to be "discovered." Europeans didn't appreciate that native peoples were already living in Africa. They didn't know—or care—that Africans had a rich way of life with their own customs, laws, arts, and governments. England, France, Spain, and other countries were looking for land to grab and call their own. This hunger for new land was called the "Scramble for Africa."

One British explorer had already been to Africa, though. His name was David Livingstone. He spent fifteen years there. Livingstone crossed the huge continent from coast to coast. At one point, he was attacked by a lion. When he came back to London, he was a hero.

In 1866, Livingstone returned to Africa to search for the source of the Nile River. This time, he was gone so long, people began to wonder about him. Was he still alive?

So the *New York Herald* newspaper decided to find out. They sent Henry Morton Stanley, their best young reporter, to Africa to find Livingstone.

Although the trip would be incredibly hard, Stanley wanted fame and glory. He hired 190 African men to help him on the trip. They carried his supplies, cooked his food, guided him through the jungle, and protected him from many dangers. But Stanley wasn't grateful. He was awful to them.

Stanley whipped the Africans to make them work harder. He forced them to walk uphill, carrying heavy loads. If they tried to run away, he chained them up like slaves. Stanley thought the Africans should be grateful to *him*!

For nearly eight months, Stanley marched toward the center of Africa. He covered seven hundred miles, mostly on foot. He nearly died from illness along the way.

Finally, on November 10, 1871, Stanley found Livingstone by Lake Tanganyika. Livingstone was ill but refused to leave because his work was not done. He died in Africa two years later.

But Stanley's eyes had been opened to the riches available in Africa.

Just across from Lake Tanganyika was the enormous area that would come to be known as the Congo.

Soon the Congo would become a prize jewel in the Scramble for Africa—and Stanley would play a big role in the shameful events that happened next.

CHAPTER 1
The Heart of Africa

In Africa, the name Congo means many things. It is the name of a huge winding river, almost three thousand miles long. It is the name of the vast river basin—the area around a river where rainfall collects and drains into the river. Congo is also part of the names of two modern-day countries. The larger one is called the Democratic Republic of the Congo. The smaller one is called the Republic of the Congo. When people say "the Congo," they sometimes mean the whole enormous area around the river and the river basin in both countries. They can also mean one of the two countries—often the larger one.

For hundreds of miles, the Congo River acts

as a border between the two countries. Shaped like a curving snake or an arch, the river flows north for hundreds of miles and crosses the equator. Then it makes a U-turn and flows south, crossing the equator again before heading out to the Atlantic Ocean. Along the way,

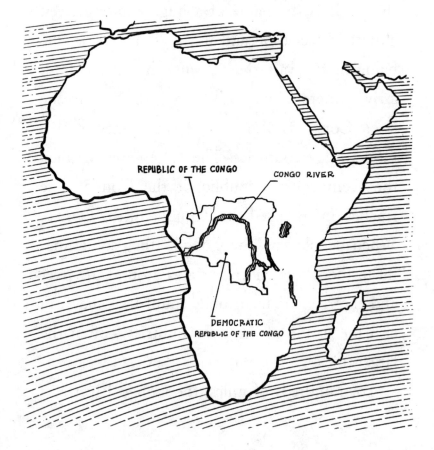

the river is dotted with waterfalls and rapids. Four main rivers, called tributaries, feed into it. The Lualaba River is the largest one.

The Congo River has many important roles to play in Central Africa. Filled with hundreds of kinds of fish, it's a source of food. Crocodiles, too.

West African crocodile

It's also a source of water for gorillas living in the rain forest nearby. And the river is like a highway running through Africa. For as long as people have built rafts and boats, they've used the river to go from place to place.

Most importantly, the Congo River acts as a drainage system for all the rain that falls in the area. And there is a huge amount of rain! The region gets about seventy-nine inches of rainfall every year. That's almost twice as much as Seattle, Washington, which is known as one of the rainiest cities in the United States.

Why is there so much rain? Because the Congo contains the second-largest rain forest in the world. Only the Amazon in South America is bigger. The rain forest is filled with a huge variety of plants and animals. There are 2,400 different kinds of orchids in African rain forests. Orchids are beautiful flowering plants. Mahogany, ebony, and palm trees grow there, too. Some

Orchid from the Congo Basin rain forest

trees in the rain forest can reach 160 feet tall. That's as tall as a sixteen-story building!

Congo Basin

In the rain forest, it can rain for days and days at a time. The Congo—and the rain forest—are both near the equator, so the weather is always warm. Warm weather makes it a perfect place for plants and animals to thrive.

The river and the rain forest cover a lot of
the Congo Basin. Other parts of the Congo
are mountainous and jagged. And some areas are
flat and covered with grasslands called savannas.
There are also active volcanoes that have erupted

several times in the past twenty years. Each type of landscape offers different advantages for the people living there.

But who lives in the Congo? And how did they find their way into the heart of Africa?

Why Is It Always Warm at the Equator?

The equator is an imaginary line that circles the middle of the globe. It is halfway between the North Pole and the South Pole.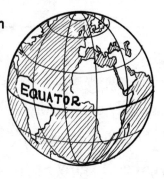

As Earth circles around the sun, it is tilted at an angle. When one part of the globe is pointed toward the sun, the weather is warmer, and it's summer. When a part of the globe is pointed away from the sun, the weather gets colder—winter. But since the equator is in the middle, it's never pointed away from the sun. So the temperature doesn't change much, and the days never get longer or shorter. The average temperature in the Congo is about seventy-five degrees Fahrenheit—a perfect summer day!

CHAPTER 2
Kingdom of Kongo

Scientists tell us that all human beings originally came from Africa.

The first people to settle in the Congo were Pygmies. Pygmy is the name for several different groups of people who are all very short. The men are less than five feet tall. Pygmies probably lived

in southern Africa for tens of thousands of years before anyone else arrived. They were hunters and gatherers—they didn't plant their own food. Instead, they lived in the rain forests and hunted animals for their meat. They also gathered whatever fruits and berries they could find to eat.

About two thousand years ago, the Bantu people showed up. Many settled

Cassava root

in the Congo Basin. The Bantu were hunters who also had farms. They grew corn, bananas, yams, and a root vegetable called cassava. Over time, they learned to use copper and iron tools.

As the Bantu people spread throughout Africa, they formed many small tribes. Each tribe had different customs and its own language. Even today there are more than two hundred different languages spoken in the Congo!

Mongo people in the Democratic Republic of the Congo

Today, about ninety-six million people live in the two countries that are both called Congo. About half a million of them are Pygmies. The rest belong to hundreds of different tribes or ethnic groups. Some of the largest groups are the Luba, Mongo, and Kongo. A small number of white people with European origins live in the Congo, too.

Hundreds of years ago, the Kongo people were the largest and most important group in that part of Africa. They created the Kingdom of Kongo (spelled with a *K*, not a *C*). The Kingdom of Kongo covered an area on the west coast of Africa that overlaps several countries today. More than two million people lived there.

KINGDOM
OF
KONGO

SOUTH ATLANTIC
OCEAN

The kingdom had existed since 1390. It had a ruler called the *manikongo*—"King of Kongo." It also had a capital city surrounded by many smaller towns and provinces. Governors were in charge of the provinces. Judges decided cases when people broke the law. The king collected taxes from his people. For money, they used cowrie shells—small shells found on an island that the king controlled.

Nzinga a Nkuwu, king of Kongo, ruled from 1470 to 1509

The king had a strong government and some very strict rules. No one was allowed to watch him eat. To approach the king, people had to crawl on all fours. His throne was made of wood and ivory. He carried a whip made from a zebra tail.

The Kongo people had no writing, but they had many other skills. They knew how to make

copper jewelry and iron tools. They grew bananas and yams. They raised cattle, pigs, and goats.

They also enslaved people.

Slavery was common in much of Africa. Usually enslaved people had been captured during a war or had committed crimes. Sometimes a woman's parents would give enslaved people to her husband as a wedding present. Sometimes enslaved people were set free after a certain number of years. And sometimes free people married people who were enslaved.

In 1482, explorers from Portugal began arriving in Kongo. Some were priests and missionaries—men who wanted to spread their Christian religion throughout the world. But others were slave traders. They came to buy Africans who were already enslaved. In exchange for these human beings, they offered jewelry, cloth, and tools.

At first, the Kongo king agreed that enslaved people could be sold to the Portuguese. But over time, the slave trade got out of control. More and more slave traders arrived. They wanted more enslaved people than there were in Kongo. So the Kongo people began capturing and selling free people. They went farther inland to the jungle and kidnapped people. Then they tied them together and marched them back to European ships waiting on the coast of Africa. By the early 1500s, more than five thousand people were being sold each year. Most were sent to Brazil.

By the 1600s, the number had tripled to more than fifteen thousand enslaved people per year. By then, many were sent to the British colonies in North America.

One Kongo king tried to stop the slave trade. His name was Afonso I. He ruled Kongo from 1509 to 1542. He had become a Catholic and had learned to read and write by studying the Bible with Portuguese priests.

King Afonso I of Kongo

Afonso wrote a letter to the king of Portugal, begging him to stop the slave trade. He explained that thousands of his people were being kidnapped, even his own nephews and grandsons. When the king wouldn't help, Afonso I wrote to the pope—the head of the Catholic Church— and pleaded with him to end the slave trade. But the slave traders made sure the letters never reached the pope.

Nothing could stop the slave trade. The African

village chiefs were getting rich by selling enslaved people. The white slave traders were getting even richer.

After Afonso died, the Kingdom of Kongo was much weaker. In 1665, Portugal fought a war against Kongo and won.

It was just the first step in the awful history that awaited many African territories. White people arrived. They had guns. They wanted new lands. And they intended to have their way.

CHAPTER 3
Stanley's Fame

Once Henry Morton Stanley found David Livingstone in Africa, his whole life changed. He became famous. He wrote a book about finding Livingstone. People in the United States and Europe wanted to hear more from Stanley and more about this continent that still seemed so mysterious to them.

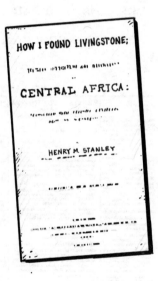

In 1874, two newspapers—one American and one British—sent Stanley back to Africa for a second trip.

This time, he hired even more Africans to

help. It was almost a small army. They carried eight tons of equipment, including rifles and ammunition. He was gone for two and a half years. He covered seven thousand miles!

During the trip, Stanley sent letters back to the newspapers in the United States and England. In his stories, he made it sound like he was a hero on a great adventure.

But the truth was different. Stanley was a harsh boss. When the African workers were too sick or tired to go on, he had them whipped.

Whenever Stanley came upon a village of people who seemed hostile, he and his men attacked them. Stanley's men had guns. The African villagers had only spears and arrows. They had never seen guns before.

As he went, Stanley named the various lakes and waterfalls for European explorers. He named an enormous series of waterfalls for himself—Stanley Falls. He also named a wide section of the Congo River for himself, calling it Stanley Pool.

Boyoma Falls, formerly known as Stanley Falls

By the end of the trip, a huge number of the African porters and guards had either died or run away. The rest were starving. Stanley was, too. He barely made it alive to Boma, a town on the west coast of Africa. Boma is near the spot where the Congo River empties into the ocean.

But Stanley did survive and arrived in England in 1878. Now he was even more famous. He wrote a book titled *Through the Dark Continent*. He began giving speeches and meeting royalty.

One king was very eager to meet Stanley.

King Leopold II of Belgium had read all about Stanley's African trip. The king had a secret plan. He wanted to grab a piece of Africa for himself— and he desperately hoped that Stanley would help him get it.

CHAPTER 4
The King Wants Cake

King Leopold II of Belgium was a greedy, power-hungry man. As king of a small country, he felt unimportant. England and France had taken some land in other parts of the world. Leopold wanted to do that, too. Maybe Africa was the place Leopold could make a fortune and build up his own little empire. Leopold called the continent a "magnificent African cake." He wanted a slice of it for himself.

King Leopold II of Belgium

Leopold knew he couldn't just take land in

Africa without a good excuse. Other countries might try to stop him.

So he came up with an idea: He would hire Stanley to go to Africa. Stanley was a famous and respected explorer. No one would suspect that he was trying to steal land for the king.

At the same time, Leopold invented stories—lies—that he hoped the rest of Europe would believe. He claimed he wanted to put an end to the slave trade in Africa. He made it sound like he was doing good work. Slavery was illegal in most of the world by this time. But Africans were still being sold as slaves to Arab countries.

Leopold knew that many Europeans would praise him—even give him money!—to end African slavery.

But Leopold had only one real reason for sending Stanley to Africa.

The king wanted to get rich.

He wanted Stanley to build roads and trading stations along the Congo River. Why? So that ivory from elephant tusks could be transported from the heart of the jungle to the west coast. From there, ships would take the ivory back to Belgium. Ivory was very valuable. It was used for piano keys, chess pieces, combs, false teeth, billiard balls, statues, jewelry, and more. The king knew he could make money selling it.

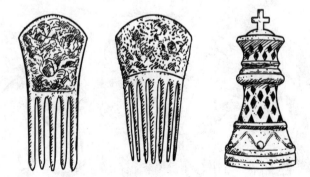

Ivory: An Elephant's Tusk

It's no longer legal to kill elephants for their ivory tusks. In 1989, most countries in the world agreed to make selling ivory illegal. And in 2018, China joined the rest of the world in trying to protect elephants.

But until those laws were passed, about one hundred thousand elephants were killed in Africa each year. In less than a hundred years, the number of elephants dropped from ten million to fewer than half a million alive today.

Even more important, the king wanted Stanley to make deals with all the village chiefs. He wanted them to agree that the king owned their land. King Leopold planned to own the Congo himself, as his own private kingdom. He wasn't even going to share it with Belgium, the country he ruled.

Stanley agreed to go.

In 1879, Stanley sailed for Africa for the third time. All his expenses were paid for by King Leopold.

For the next five years, Stanley and his men hacked their way through the Congo. They built trading stations. The stations were a collection of buildings grouped together where white men could live and do business with the Africans. This time, Stanley named everything in sight after King Leopold II. The biggest trading station was called Léopoldville. Lakes, rivers, and hills were named for the king, too.

Stanley met with 450 village chiefs and got them to sign treaties—agreements between the chiefs and the king. However, the chiefs couldn't read or write, so they didn't understand the deals. They signed the treaties with an X. In the treaties, the chiefs agreed to give up their land and to only do business with King Leopold. In return, all they were given were a few pieces of cloth or some coats and a few bottles of gin.

The "Scramble for Africa" was on.

Soon, other European countries made claims to land in Africa. A French explorer named Pierre de Brazza claimed land north of the Congo River for France. Eventually, that land would become the

Pierre de Brazza

country known as the Republic of the Congo. Great Britain and Portugal claimed land, too. Leopold had to hurry if he wanted a big slice of the African cake.

Once he had all the signed treaties, Leopold had one last job. He had to get the rest of the world—especially Europe and the United States—to agree that all the Congo region south of the river belonged to him.

Treaties

Treaties are signed agreements between two or more countries. Sometimes a treaty is an agreement to end a war. In 1783, England signed a treaty to end the American Revolutionary War. The king agreed to give up power over the thirteen colonies in North America. They were now the United States, an independent country.

Other treaties are offers to buy land. In 1867, the United States signed a treaty with Russia to buy Alaska for more than seven million dollars. The US government also signed many treaties with American Indian tribes. Those agreements bought land from the Native Americans but gave them very little in return.

Signing of the treaty to end the American Revolutionary War, 1783

For this, Leopold got the help of an American friend named Henry Shelton Sanford. Sanford was very well known in Washington, DC. He convinced the president and people in Congress that Leopold was trying to end slavery in the Congo. He got newspapers to write stories saying that King Leopold was a hero. Sanford promised Americans that Leopold's Congo

Henry Shelton Sanford

would be a "free state"—meaning that the people would be free.

It all sounded so good that the United States agreed to recognize the Congo Free State as a new country. Pretty soon, France and Germany agreed, too.

On May 29, 1885, Leopold declared himself the king of the Congo Free State.

But the people in the Congo were not free. Far from it. The rest of the world didn't know it yet, but the Congolese people would be forced to work for a cruel, brutal king who claimed he owned all their villages. The Congolese were practically enslaved.

CHAPTER 5
Slave Labor

Before King Leopold could begin taking huge loads of ivory out of the Congo, he needed to build a railroad.

The Congo River was like a highway winding all through the Congo Basin. Ships could sail for many miles up and down the river, transporting

goods. But sections of the river with waterfalls and rapids were too dangerous. If boats sailed over the edge of a waterfall, they would crash. So in these areas, the king built a railroad that followed alongside the river. It wound 220 miles around the rapids.

He set up Boma as the capital city of the Congo Free State. At trading stations, he built small towns with white men as the governors. The white officials had fancy teacups and furniture. They dressed in suits and ties every day. They ate marmalade and drank expensive wines.

But the Africans lived a very different life.

There were only two kinds of jobs for Africans in the Congo Free State. They could either be part of the police force and army—or they could do miserable, backbreaking labor.

At first, most workers had to carry heavy loads of goods, tools, boats, and elephant tusks for miles and miles. Later, they were put to work building the railroad. The workers were given very little pay—only food or bits of cloth and beads.

If they tried to escape, they were whipped and then chained at the neck. Many African workers starved to death or died from their cruel treatment.

As for the army, black soldiers had to work under white officers who were in charge. Their job was to force other Africans to work. They treated the workers brutally.

The army was filled with Africans who would rather be on the king's side—holding the guns and whips—than on the other side, being beaten.

King Leopold made all this happen without ever setting foot in Africa himself.

The police force, called the Force Publique, punished anyone who didn't do what they were told. Sometimes they kidnapped women and children from a village and held them hostage. They took all the chickens and food. No one could get anything to eat unless they obeyed the

Force Publique. The village men had to work for free in order to get their families back.

At other times, the police simply bought men from the village chiefs. Or they kidnapped the men and took them far away.

Why Congolese People Speak French

The Congo Free State police force was called the Force Publique—a French term for "public force." When King Leopold took over the Congo, French was the most common language spoken in Belgium. French became the language used by most Europeans who settled in the Congo.

Today, French is still the official language of the Democratic Republic of the Congo. It is used along with four native languages: Swahili, Lingala, Kongo, and Tshiluba. French is also spoken in the smaller Congo country, the Republic of the Congo.

(English) (French) (Swahili)
country = pays = nchi

Chokwe tribe members

By the year 1900, there were nineteen thousand officers and men working in the king's police force. Without guns, how could the villagers fight back? Still, sometimes Africans did rebel. The Chokwe tribe waged war for twenty years against Leopold's soldiers. But in the end, the army had more weapons. The Force Publique always won.

At first, ivory was the main thing that King Leopold took from the Congo. But by the late 1890s, the king discovered a new way to make money—from rubber!

Rubber vines grew wild in the jungles of Africa. And rubber was suddenly very valuable to the world. It was used for a new invention—tires! It was also great for rubber boots, raincoats, hoses, and much more.

Rubber vines in the Congo Basin

The Man Who Invented Bicycle Tires

In 1888, an Irishman named John Dunlop figured out a way to make bicycles more  fun to ride—by making better tires. Until then, bicycles had wooden or metal wheels wrapped in a solid band of rubber. The ride was very bumpy and uncomfortable. It gave John Dunlop's young son headaches. So Dunlop put an inflatable rubber tire on his son's tricycle to cushion the ride. The air-filled tires were so much better, they started a bicycle craze. Soon, bicycle clubs and bicycle races sprang up all over the United States and Great Britain. The demand for rubber exploded. Today, the Dunlop brand still makes tires for bicycles and cars. They make tennis balls, too.

Leopold wanted as much rubber from the Congo as he could get. It was worth a lot more than ivory. So he forced Africans to collect it from the jungles.

Almost all natural rubber is made from a runny white liquid in the rubber plant, called latex. In the Congo, wild rubber vines grew through trees that were almost a hundred feet tall! To get the rubber out, workers had to cut a slit in the vine and let the thick, gooey latex drip into a bucket. When the vines near the ground were drained dry, men climbed up into the trees and cut into branches for more latex. It was dangerous work—sometimes men fell and got hurt.

Once the rubber vines near the villages were drained, the men went deeper into the jungle to search for fresh vines. Sometimes they had to walk for two days to find them. The men hated the work, but they couldn't refuse.

Collecting natural latex from a rubber tree

Their families were being held hostage until they came back with enough latex.

It was a miserable life for the people of the Congo Free State. Their country had been taken from them. They were dying under a terrible, brutal rule. And the rest of the world had no idea this was happening.

Would anyone ever find out the truth?

CHAPTER 6
Speaking Truth to the King

One man had been to the Congo and hated how Africans were being treated. His name was George Washington Williams, and he was a black American.

George Washington Williams

Williams was a brilliant man with many talents. At the time when slavery was just ending in the United States, he became a minister, newspaperman, lawyer, and public speaker. Later, he met several presidents of the United States.

One day, Williams heard about King Leopold's new country, the Congo Free State. So he decided to go there and find out what it was like. Williams thought it might be a good place for black Americans to live and work.

Williams went to Belgium first and talked to King Leopold. He was dazzled by the king. He thought the Congo must be wonderful.

Then he went to Africa to see it for himself.

What he found was a horror. He saw Africans treated like they were enslaved. There were no schools or hospitals. He saw white officers shoot at Congolese people just for fun—as if it were target practice.

Williams sat down and began writing "An Open Letter to His Serene Majesty Leopold II." In the letter, Williams listed all the crimes the king was committing against human beings.

His "open letter" was soon printed in pamphlets and newspapers all over Europe and the United States. The king quickly and furiously denied the stories.

Some people believed what Williams had written. But many people believed the king. The king's powerful friends all defended him. Soon after the letter's publication, Williams became very ill and died later that year.

Did anything change after Williams wrote his letter to the king?

No. In fact, things got worse. Thousands more people were worked to death.

It would be ten more years before another brave voice would cry out about the horrors in the Congo Free State. That brave voice came from Edmund Morel.

Morel was a young man in his midtwenties who had grown up in France and England. He worked in Belgium for a shipping company.

Edmund Morel

His job was to check on supplies that were being sent to the Congo.

Morel began to notice some things that were very strange. Most of the supplies that were being sent to Africa were guns and ammunition. Why?

Then there was another question: How was the king paying workers for all the ivory and rubber? People in the Congo didn't use money the way Europeans did. They traded. But the king wasn't sending goods to trade—such as cloth or tools that the Congolese would want. So how was he paying the workers?

Morel figured out the truth: The king's officers weren't paying workers for the rubber. They were using all those guns to force the Congolese people to work.

Morel was outraged. He felt he had uncovered a deep, dark secret. It was like discovering a murder—except it wasn't just one murder. It was thousands!

When Morel reported the facts, his boss tried to shut him up with a bribe. Morel refused.

Instead, he quit his job and spent the next ten years letting the world know about these crimes. At the age of thirty, he started his own newspaper in England. He wrote stories and books about King Leopold's Congo. He made speeches all over the world. As many as five thousand people showed up to hear him speak. Pretty soon, other people began to tell Morel their own stories about the Congo. They wrote letters and sent photographs

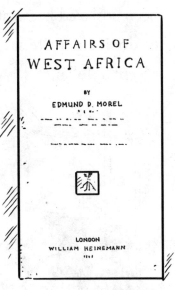

describing the horrible deeds they witnessed there.

In 1904, Morel started an organization called the Congo Reform Association (CRA). Its purpose was to speak out against King Leopold's brutal rule.

The CRA raised large sums of money for the cause. At one rally, a woman became so upset that she took off her jewelry and gave it to the CRA. In the United States, a woman who had once been enslaved heard about the Congo—and tried to donate her life savings! The CRA would only accept a dollar.

Morel went to Washington, DC, and met President Theodore Roosevelt. Morel said the United States should take the lead in ending King Leopold's rule because it was partly to blame for the Congo. Why? Because the United States had been the first country to accept King Leopold's claim to the Congo.

Through all this, Leopold did everything he could to keep the story quiet. The king bribed newspapers to say Morel's stories were wrong.

For a while, it worked. But finally a big New York newspaper learned all about the bribes. They printed the story. Now the world knew the whole truth. As many as ten million people had died while Leopold owned the Congo—just so the king could make himself rich.

To make things right, everyone agreed Leopold had to give up the Congo.

But no one considered letting the people of the Congo rule themselves. White people were prejudiced against black people. They thought Africans weren't capable of running the country themselves. It would take many more years for those ideas to change.

Instead, most people agreed that Belgium should take over. So Leopold sold the Congo to Belgium—and got rich all over again. He got money that would be worth more than a billion dollars today. He died a year later.

In November 1908, the Congo Free State officially became a possession of Belgium. But it was a long way from being truly free.

CHAPTER 7
One Country, Many Names

For the next fifty-two years, the Congo Free State had a new name. It was called the Belgian Congo.

Life was supposed to get better for the Congolese people with Leopold gone and the country of Belgium in charge. But it didn't really.

Now the Congolese had to pay taxes to the Belgian government. They were still forced to work in jobs they didn't want to do. They worked on rubber plantations—big farms where rubber trees were grown. They also worked in gold, copper, and tin mines. Villagers were often rounded up, chained together, and marched off to the mines against their will. They were still whipped if they tried to escape or disobeyed.

In the 1920s, big businesses from all over the world arrived in the Congo. One company was owned by Englishman William Lever. He planted palm trees and sold palm oil. Belgians, French, and Americans owned diamond, copper, and gold mining companies. From the early twentieth century through the present day, big companies

were given rights to do business in the Congo. In exchange, the companies built schools and hospitals. They built roads and more railroads. But they did it the same way as before—by forcing Africans to work and taking away their freedom.

During World War II, however, things began to change.

World War II

World War II started in 1939 when Germany invaded Poland. In 1940, Italy joined the war on Germany's side. Germany and Italy were defeated by a group of countries called the Allies, led by Great Britain, Russia, and the United States (which entered the war in late 1941). The war ended in 1945.

German soldiers invading Poland, 1939

Belgium was on the side of the Allies in the war. When the war spread to northern Africa, men from the Congo were sent to join the Belgian army there. They fought alongside soldiers from England and France. They saw that other soldiers weren't whipped or flogged. Other soldiers were treated well and paid. The Congolese soldiers wanted the same kind of life.

By the late 1950s, other African countries were gaining their independence. The area north of the Congo River had never been owned by Leopold or Belgium. It was a French-owned territory—part of what was called French Equatorial Africa. In 1958, France gave the people the vote and changed the name of the country to the Republic of the Congo.

Now people in the Belgian Congo were ready to fight for their independence, too. And they had the right man to lead them.

His name was Patrice Lumumba.

Lumumba was a brilliant young man who had learned to speak many languages. He wrote poetry and read books by great thinkers from Europe while working in the post office in Stanleyville.

In 1958, Lumumba helped start a political group that wanted the Congo to be free. He stirred up people with speeches. He said freedom wasn't a gift—it was a right. Huge crowds of people showed up to hear him speak. His group and others marched and protested. In January 1959, riots broke out in the streets in Léopoldville. Finally, Belgium agreed to let the Congolese people have the vote.

Patrice Lumumba

Lumumba signs the Act of Independence

When the country held elections in May 1960, Patrice Lumumba won. He was elected as the first prime minister of the new country. On June 30, 1960, the Belgian Congo changed its name to the Republic of the Congo, and Belgium was no longer in charge. For a while, there were two countries with the exact same name!

Lumumba was an inspiring leader. The new country, however, was too young to be stable. Soon, Patrice Lumumba's enemies began a struggle for power. They had Lumumba arrested—and killed by a firing squad.

Beginning in 1965, the former Belgian Congo was ruled for the next thirty-two years by a harsh dictator named Mobutu Sese Seko. Mobutu was just like King Leopold in some ways—cruel and greedy. During Mobutu's rule, the country fell apart. The army wasn't paid, and the garbage wasn't collected. Some parts of the country were at war with other parts. There were riots in the streets.

Mobutu Sese Seko

Mobutu changed the name of the country again. First it was called the Democratic Republic of the Congo (DRC). Then he changed it to the Republic of Zaire. The names of the cities were changed, too. Léopoldville, which was now the capital city, became Kinshasa.

Several US presidents thought Mobutu was the right man to be in charge of the Congo because he was friendly toward the United States. So the United States gave him a billion dollars in aid. The money was supposed to be for the people of the Congo and for the army. But Mobutu stole a huge amount for himself. He bought a yacht and several huge mansions in Europe. He took big bribes from companies doing business in the country.

Finally, in 1997, Mobutu was forced out. Armies from two neighboring countries— Rwanda and Uganda—had invaded Zaire. A man named Laurent Kabila declared himself president.

Laurent Kabila inspecting troops

The country's name was changed back to the DRC.

But the Congo was still not a peaceful place. Different groups were still fighting for power and for control of the country's riches—diamonds, oil, cobalt, and gold. Small armies of rebels roamed the countryside. Civil war broke out between the DRC army, the rebels, and the Rwandans.

President Kabila was assassinated in 2001. His son Joseph took over, but the new president changed nothing.

For years afterward, the Congo was filled with misery, war, and violence. Even today, the Congo is still one of the most dangerous places on earth. The civil wars continue. Many people are sick and starving. The government doesn't seem willing or able to bring peace. The United Nations—an organization of nearly all the countries of the world—sends troops to the Congo as peacekeepers. But even those peacekeepers are at risk of being hurt.

Still, there is one part of the Congo where life is green and peaceful: the jungle and the rain forest.

CHAPTER 8
Jungle Life

Imagine a forest so big, it covers almost a third of the United States. Miles and miles of thick, dense trees reach over a hundred feet tall. Under the giant treetops lives a world of wonderful plants and animals. There are a thousand different kinds of birds. Two thousand kinds of butterflies.

Ten thousand kinds of plants. Great apes roam through the mountains and rain forests. African elephants live in the forests as well.

Elephants are the largest walking animals on earth. There are two types in the Congo Basin. One type lives on the savannas—the grassy flatlands. The savanna elephants weigh about six tons. That's more than two pickup trucks! Forest elephants live in the rain forest and are a bit smaller.

Savanna elephant

Forest elephant

Elephants are some of the most interesting animals on the planet. They live up to seventy years—almost as long as people live. They live in groups and take care of their babies for a long time, like humans do. When an elephant dies, the rest of its family pays careful attention to the body and bones. Animal experts have noticed that elephants seem to recognize the bones of their ancestors. They'll turn the bones over, almost as if they get comfort from doing this.

How do they turn the bones over? With their trunks!

An elephant's trunk is an amazing tool— almost like a hand, arm, nose, and mouth all rolled into one. There are more than one hundred thousand muscles in the trunk. An elephant could use its trunk to lift a five-hundred-pound refrigerator!

But they can also do very delicate work with their trunks. There are two flaps at the end of the trunk, almost like fingers or lips. With those flaps, an elephant can crack open a peanut, blow away the shell, and then eat the tiny nut.

Elephants use their trunks for many things. They grab leaves and other food with their trunks, then stick them into their mouths. They scratch themselves with their trunks. They also use their trunks to touch other elephants on their faces.

Or to "shake hands" by wrapping their trunks around another elephant's trunk. They use their trunks like a vacuum cleaner to suck up water and then shoot it into their mouths. Sometimes elephants suck up dust and then blow it onto themselves, to shoo away insects.

On top of all that, they use their trunks to breathe!

Tusks are another useful tool. Elephants use them to dig in the dirt. And sometimes males will use their tusks when fighting each other. Their tusks stick out enough to protect them if another elephant comes charging.

Even though selling ivory is now illegal, some people still shoot elephants for the ivory. Also, some Congolese people are so hungry that they shoot elephants for the meat. When wild animals are killed for food, it's called "bushmeat."

Bushmeat isn't legal, and it isn't safe. It can carry diseases. But in the Congo, meat is scarce and many people are hungry. Millions of tons of bushmeat are sold in markets every year. So elephants need to be protected. The national parks are supposed to keep them safe, but it is difficult and dangerous to stop people from hunting illegally.

Gorillas and chimpanzees are plentiful in the rain forests of the Congo. The largest of the great apes is the gorilla. The males weigh up to 485 pounds—more than twice as much as an average adult man. They're not as tall as most men, though.

They stand only about four to five and a half feet tall on their back legs. They can stand upright, like people, but they walk on all fours. Their arms are actually longer than their legs! Gorillas walk with their weight on the knuckles of their hands. It's called knuckle-walking.

Gorillas live in family groups with the males in charge. In the daytime, they search for food—

leaves, stalks, and fruit. At night, each gorilla makes a quick nest out of branches, either on the ground or in trees.

Gorillas are usually shy—they don't go looking for trouble. But if someone threatens them, they'll put on a huge show of strength. They'll beat their chests, pound the earth, and make terrifying noises. The roar of a large male gorilla is enough to scare off almost anyone who comes near.

Virunga Mountains

Most mountain gorillas live in the Virunga Mountains, smack in the center of Africa. Other kinds of gorillas live in the "lowlands" of the rain forest—the flatter areas.

All gorillas are in serious danger of becoming extinct. Gorillas are hunted in the Congo as bushmeat. They are also in trouble because the trees and forests where they live are being cut down. Africans are cutting down rain forests so they can plant food instead.

The same problems affect another Congo ape—the chimpanzee.

Chimpanzees are smaller than the gorillas, and they're even more social—they like hanging out in groups. A male is in charge of the group. Chimps do many of the same things that people do. They share and take care of each other, but they also sometimes fight. They adopt babies whose parents have died, but they also tease and play tricks on one another.

They wipe their mouths after they've eaten, and they clean each other. They also know how to use tools—ropes and sticks—to break things and dig holes to find food.

Scientists have taught chimps to use sign language—hand and finger gestures that stand for words. (Gorillas can learn sign language, too.)

Chimps are so much like human beings because we have almost the same DNA—the code in our genes that determines how we look, act, and feel. They are our closest relatives in the animal world.

One of the most unusual animals found in the Congo rain forest is the bonobo. Like chimps, bonobos have almost the same DNA as humans. But bonobos are very rare. They live in the Congo and nowhere else on earth. Bonobos are smaller than chimps and more peaceful. Instead of being ruled by males, they are led by the females in the group. Bonobos almost never fight. They are so friendly, they often kiss each other!

Female bonobo

Bonobos and chimps are listed as endangered species by the World Wildlife Fund. That means that these animals could become extinct if we don't protect them. In the Congo, people hunt chimps for bushmeat. They also try to capture them and sell them as pets or to zoos.

But being hunted isn't the only problem for the animals of the Congo. Their homes are in danger of disappearing.

Why would anyone want to destroy a beautiful old forest?

CHAPTER 9
Saving the Congo

In recent years, many people have been cutting down the old trees in the rain forests. Some cut down the trees to use as firewood. Others have been clearing the forests so they can plant a different kind of tree.

What? Why would anyone cut down old trees to plant new ones?

It sounds very confusing, but it's true. Big companies make a lot of money selling palm oil. The oil comes from the palm tree fruit. It is used as a cooking oil and as an ingredient in many foods. It's also used in cosmetics and sometimes as a fuel for trucks or trains.

A palm oil plantation

So forests are cleared to make way for palm trees. But palm trees aren't as good for the environment as the rain forests are. Rain forests are not only a habitat for animals. They are much more than that. They play an important role in keeping the entire planet healthy.

There are other problems with planting palm trees. The land used for palm trees is often land that should have been returned to the people who lived there over a hundred years ago—when King Leopold took over.

The World Wildlife Fund and other groups are working to make people realize that cutting down the rain forests is a bad idea. They also hope people will turn away from palm oil. If people stop buying palm oil, then maybe the old trees won't be cut down.

Women selling palm oil

Rain Forests and Climate Change

Scientists know that Earth's climate is changing and getting warmer. One cause is too much carbon dioxide in the atmosphere—the layer of gases that surrounds our planet. Carbon dioxide is a gas given off by all living, breathing beings. It is also produced when we burn oil, coal, or wood.

How do rain forests help cut down on carbon dioxide in the atmosphere? Plants and trees give off oxygen—the gas all living beings need to breathe. But they also take in, or absorb, carbon dioxide. Older trees, like the ones in rain forests, take in more carbon dioxide than younger trees. Rain forests are sort of like giant sponges, soaking up carbon dioxide from the air. They have a positive effect on climate all over Earth.

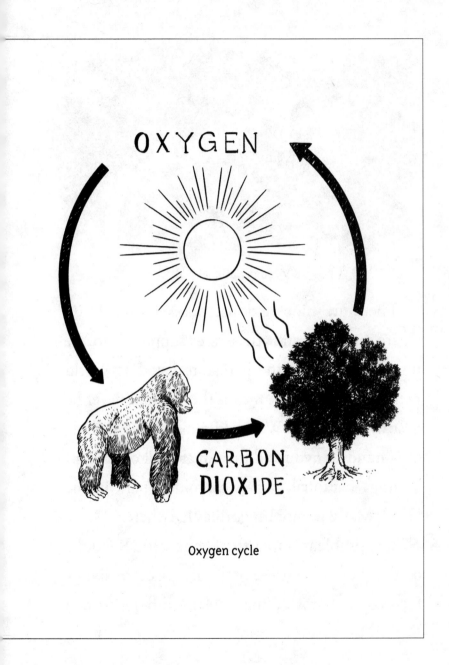

OXYGEN

CARBON
DIOXIDE

Oxygen cycle

Virunga National Park

There are nine national parks in the DRC where animals and trees are supposed to be protected. Five of the parks are listed as World Heritage Sites, which means they should never be destroyed. (Other World Heritage Sites include the Grand Canyon and the Great Wall of China.) Virunga National Park is the oldest park in the DRC. Many mountain gorillas live there.

The problem is that the Democratic Republic of the Congo is still not a safe place to live—for people or for animals. Many different small armies roam through the country. Some are rebels at war with one another. Others are at war with nearby countries. They don't let anyone stand in their way.

Even in the national parks, the animals are at risk of being killed. They are killed for bushmeat or taken by poachers who want to sell the animals.

The park rangers—the people who are there to guard the park and the animals—are in danger, too. Sometimes they are attacked by the rebel armies. In recent years, some national parks have had to close because they are too dangerous.

The troubles in the Congo started many years ago—when King Leopold stole the villagers' land.

Still, the Congo remains one of the richest places on earth—rich in terms of mineral wealth. The gold, copper, diamonds, and other precious metals in the earth are incredibly valuable. The Congo also has a good supply of a metal called coltan. Coltan is used in cell phones, computers, and electric car batteries.

Coltan   Cell phone

With so much wealth in its earth, the DRC should be able to feed its people. Instead, many people are hungry. Diseases are common. There aren't enough doctors to care for the sick.

There aren't enough police to keep people safe. And the population is exploding. Most women have four or five children. Today, nearly half of the people in the DRC are children under fifteen years old!

Will the riches of the Congo ever be used to serve the people of the Congo themselves?

And what will it take to bring this beautiful country back from the edge of disaster?

Timeline of the Congo

C. 1	Bantu people settle in the Congo Basin
1390	Kingdom of Kongo is created
1482	Portuguese explorers arrive in Kongo
1665	Portugal defeats Kongo in war
1878	King Leopold II asks Henry Morton Stanley to explore Africa
1885	Leopold II declares himself king of Congo Free State
1904	Edmund Morel starts Congo Reform Association (CRA)
1908	The country is renamed the Belgian Congo
1960	The Belgian Congo gains independence, and Patrice Lumumba is elected prime minister
1961	Lumumba is killed
1964	Former Belgian Congo name changed to the Democratic Republic of the Congo (DRC)
1965	Mobutu Sese Seko becomes ruler of the DRC
1997	Mobutu is forced out; Laurent Kabila declares himself president
1998	Civil war breaks out
2001	Kabila is assassinated by a bodyguard

Timeline of the World

1440–1450	Johannes Gutenberg invents movable type printing
1619	First slaves arrive in North America from Africa
1803	The United States buys a huge territory from France, the Louisiana Purchase
1863	President Lincoln signs the Emancipation Proclamation, freeing US slaves
1888	Inflatable rubber bicycle tires are invented
1896	The first modern Olympic Games are held in Athens, Greece
1903	Wright brothers make the first successful powered flight
1920	Women gain the right to vote in the United States
1959	Alaska and Hawaii become US states
1960	John F. Kennedy elected president of the United States
1968	Dr. Martin Luther King Jr. is assassinated
1969	US astronauts land on the moon
1973	The United States passes the Endangered Species Act to protect wildlife
1989	Sale of ivory is banned throughout most of the world
1991	The United States invades Iraq as part of the Persian Gulf War

Bibliography

"Africa : Congo, Democratic Republic of the—The World Factbook."
Central Intelligence Agency. Last modified August 13,
2019. https://www.cia.gov/library/publications/the-world-
factbook/geos/cg.html.

"Congo, Democratic Republic - Oil and Gas." **Export.gov**.
Last modified July 20, 2017. https://www.export.gov/
article?id=Congo-Democratic-Republic-Oil-and-Gas.

"David Livingstone." *Encyclopaedia Britannica Online.* Last
modified August 16, 2019. https://www.britannica.com/
biography/David-Livingstone.

"Democratic Republic of the Congo." *Encyclopaedia Britannica
Online.* Last modified July 30, 2019. https://www.britannica.
com/place/Democratic-Republic-of-the-Congo/.

Dugard, Martin. "Stanley Meets Livingstone." *Smithsonian.*
October 2003. https://www.smithsonianmag.com/history/
stanley-meets-livingstone-91118102/.

Gondola, Ch. Didier. *The History of Congo.* Westport, CT:
Greenwood Pres, 2002.

"Henry Morton Stanley." *Encyclopaedia Britannica Online.*
Last modified August 7, 2019. https://www.britannica.com/
biography/Henry-Morton-Stanley.

Hochschild, Adam. *King Leopold's Ghost.* New York: Houghton
Mifflin Harcourt, 1998.

Oregon State University. "Old Growth Forests Are Valuable Carbon
Sinks." **ScienceDaily**. September 14, 2008. https://www.
sciencedaily.com/releases/2008/09/080910133934.htm.

"Republic of the Congo." *Encyclopaedia Britannica Online.* Last
modified July 30, 2019. https://www.britannica.com/place/
Republic-of-the-Congo.

Website

www.wwf-congobasin.org

YOUR HEADQUARTERS FOR HISTORY

Activities, Mad Libs, and sidesplitting jokes!
Discover the Who HQ books beyond the biographies

Who? What? Where?

Learn more at whohq.com!